SOUTH AFRICA
A GLORIOUS COUNTRY

SOUTH AFRICA
A GLORIOUS COUNTRY

a celebration in photographs of a fascinating land and its people

wilf nussey

southwater

This edition is published by Southwater

Southwater is an imprint of Anness Publishing Ltd
Hermes House, 88-89 Blackfriars Road, London SE1 8HA
tel. 020 7401 2077; fax 020 7633 9499
www.southwaterbooks.com; info@anness.com

UK agent: The Manning Partnership Ltd, 6 The Old Dairy,
Melcombe Road, Bath BA2 3LR; tel. 01225 478444; fax 01225 478440;
sales@manning-partnership.co.uk

UK distributor: Grantham Book Services Ltd, Isaac Newton Way,
Alma Park Industrial Estate, Grantham, Lincs NG31 9SD;
tel. 01476 541080; fax 01476 541061; orders@gbs.tbs-ltd.co.uk

North American agent/distributor: National Book Network,
4501 Forbes Boulevard, Suite 200, Lanham, MD 20706;
tel. 301 459 3366; fax 301 429 5746; www.nbnbooks.com

Australian agent/distributor: Pan Macmillan Australia, Level 18,
St Martins Tower, 31 Market St, Sydney, NSW 2000; tel. 1300 135 113;
fax 1300 135 103; customer.service@macmillan.com.au

New Zealand agent/distributor: David Bateman Ltd, 30 Tarndale Grove,
Off Bush Road, Albany, Auckland; tel. (09) 415 7664; fax (09) 415 8892

A CIP catalogue record for this book is available from the British Library.

Previously published as *South Africa: A Wonderful Land*

10 9 8 7 6 5 4 3 2 1

CONTENTS

INTRODUCTION

BORN OF CONQUEST AND SHAPED BY CONFLICT, South Africa has at last reached a maturity that holds the promise of a stable future. That so bizarre an amalgam of peoples and cultures with so turbulent a past is holding together so well indicates that the country is unlikely to go the way of most of Africa. Although more than three centuries of confrontation have left South Africa with enormous social imbalances, it has abundant talent, a modern infrastructure, great economic potential and an entrenched democracy.

Of the estimated 44.8 million South Africans, more than three-quarters are blacks belonging to two main ethnic groups and nine language groups, the largest being Zulu and Xhosa. They span the full social spectrum, from illiterate rural dwellers to people at the highest levels in government, business and academia. Whites form about ten per cent of the population and are mainly of Dutch and English descent, with French,

***ABOVE** The first European to land in the Cape was the Portuguese navigator Bartolomeu Dias, in 1488, naming it the "Cape of Good Hope". He landed at what is now Mossel Bay in the Western Cape and bartered sheep and cattle from Khoi herdsmen. The honour of being the first to circumnavigate Africa, however, belongs to Phoenician sailors, who did it over several years in about 600BC.*

***LEFT** Explorers sent out by Portugal's Prince Henry the Navigator pioneered the spice trading route around Africa to India in frail caravels like this one, a reconstruction presented to South Africa by Portugal. It is now in the museum at Mossel Bay.*

ABOVE The plaque marks a huge, gnarled milkwood tree in Mossel Bay as a national monument. On 7 July 1501, Captain João da Nova sheltered in the bay after most of his fleet had sunk in a storm. He left a report about it in an old shoe hanging from the tree and for many years afterwards passing navigators left messages and mail for each other there. The tree is now an official post office and letters mailed from it are specially franked.

German, Portuguese and Jewish minority groups. About eight per cent are people of mixed blood (or Coloureds) – European, Malay, Khoi, Asian and African. Some three per cent are from India, mostly Hindu.

In 1488, a decade before Columbus reached South America, Portuguese navigators seeking a trade route to the East first encountered the inhabitants of the southern tip of Africa: the pastoral Khoi (Hottentot) and hunter-gatherer San (Bushmen) peoples. By that time blacks who had migrated from East and Central Africa, reaching the Eastern Cape in about AD700, had been co-existing with the Khoi for centuries.

The first Europeans to settle in South Africa were the Dutch, who arrived at Table Bay in 1652. They were joined 36 years later by French Huguenot refugees. In 1795 Britain

LEFT Ox-drawn wagons were to the South African hinterland what "prairie schooners" were to the American West. This one in the Voortrekker ("pioneer") Museum in Pietermaritzburg, KwaZulu/Natal, was used in the Great Trek of the early 19th century. In these sturdy vehicles Afrikaners crossed mountains and deserts to trek as far north as Kenya.

occupied the Cape to prevent Napoleon from doing so, returned it to Dutch control in 1802 and then colonized it in 1806.

Whites migrating inland by ox-wagon met the black people in the Eastern Cape for the first time in about 1770, triggering a series of nine frontier wars which spanned nearly a century. In 1820, in an attempt to end these wars, Britain sent 4,000 English men, women and children to settle in the Eastern Cape to act as a buffer between the warring groups. In 1824 more Britons settled in what became Natal, German settlers reached the Eastern Cape in 1858, and Indians began to arrive in Natal in 1860 to work in the canefields.

LEFT In the Anglo-Boer War Britain lost a series of battles against the Afrikaners in January 1900 during what became known as "Black Week". One was the Battle of Spioenkop ("spy hill") on 24 January, when General Louis Botha defeated Sir Redvers Buller. A monument marks the scene of the battle.

From about 1830, Afrikaners who had grown disenchanted with British rule in the Cape started migrating inland. The Great Trek, as it became known, lasted some 20 years. The trekkers found the interior swept almost empty by years of massive social upheaval called the Mfecane or Difaqane which had started in about 1818 when the military genius, Shaka, began conquering his neighbours and building his Zulu nation. The ripples of violence spread across most of southern Africa, creating loose rabbles who plundered everyone in their paths.

Into this semi-vacuum moved the trekkers, clashing with some black groups, protecting others. They crushed the Zulu might at the Battle of Blood River in 1838, and created the Orange Free State Republic in 1854 and the Transvaal republic in 1857.

By this time Britain had become worried about the Afrikaner threat to its power. It had expanded the Cape Colony, colonized Natal and then, for a short period, annexed the Orange Free State. But when it annexed the Transvaal in 1877 the Afrikaners rose in revolt, and in the first Anglo-Boer war in 1881 they defeated the British at Majuba Hill.

Now more powerful forces came into play, following the discovery of vast deposits of diamonds and gold in the Cape and Transvaal. Foreign greed soon overwhelmed the Transvaal, plunging it and the Orange Free State into the "Boer War" (or 1899–1902 South African War). The heavily outnumbered Afrikaners fought with skill and determination, but finally succumbed to the British forces' scorched earth policy.

ABOVE Near Ladysmith in KwaZulu/Natal, a lonely row of English graves in quiet countryside bears testimony to the violence that erupted here two weeks after the Anglo-Boer War began. At the ferocious Battle of Elandslaagte ("eland hollow") British lancers inflicted a resounding defeat on the Afrikaners.

ABOVE As dusk closes in, the lights of Cape Town come glitteringly alive in the distance. This view from Robben Island ("Seal Island") must have saddened the political prisoners, including Nelson Mandela, incarcerated on the island by the apartheid regime.

ABOVE A joyous Nelson Mandela greets the huge crowd in Cape Town who came to welcome him soon after his release from 27 years in prison. With him is Winnie Mandela, whom he divorced after he became President of South Africa.

ABOVE The general election in April 1994, which ushered in a democratic South Africa, was a first for blacks and a novelty for whites, too, who found themselves queuing with their servants to cast their votes. Contrary to widespread fears, the election was remarkably peaceful.

In 1910 Britain created the Union of South Africa, uniting the Cape, Natal, the Orange Free State and Transvaal under one government – but only for whites. Throughout South African history black and coloured people had been denied equal rights, except in the Cape where there was a small measure of equality. White rulers adopted a paternalistic attitude towards non-whites, ignoring the rising number who matched them in skills and intellect. Growing dissatisfaction among non-whites led to the formation, in 1912, of the African National Congress (ANC).

Tentative moves by the whites to improve the lot of the blacks came to an abrupt halt in 1948 when Afrikaner nationalists unexpectedly won the general election. They launched apartheid ("apartness"), one of man's uglier forms of repression. As anger and resentment grew among the usually passive, easy-going black people, the National Party government resorted to ever more brutal means of suppressing them. In its last decade of power the National Party government abandoned all semblance of democracy, carried devastating war into neighbouring countries and oppressed all internal opposition

LEFT After President F.W. de Klerk announced the demise of apartheid in February 1990, the artificial taboos of race disappeared with hardly a ripple. People could live normal lives, like this couple in Soweto, the city south-west of Johannesburg formerly reserved for blacks.

so harshly that it turned South Africa into a time bomb.

President F.W. de Klerk defused the bomb on 2 February 1990. He lifted the ban on the ANC and, two weeks later, Nelson Mandela was freed, opening the way to the general election in April 1994 when, for the first time, all South Africans were eligible to vote. The new nation confounded the world by emerging in peace. It has some localized political conflict, it has crime, it has many other problems. But it is here to stay.

LEFT Discriminatory barriers — of gender as well as of race — are coming down throughout the new South Africa. Here, a black woman and a white man discuss a business deal in Johannesburg, the economic heart of South Africa.

ABOVE Black women, whom many describe as the backbone of South Africa, form a large part of the workforce and do much of the basic labour. This woman is harvesting red and green peppers on a farm near Johannesburg.

1

LANDSCAPE

A STUDY OF SOUTH AFRICA'S GEOLOGY is like a journey in a time machine. Its 1,219,090 square kilometres (about 471,000 square miles) encompass most of the Earth's geological history, from the birth of the land mass some 4.5 billion years ago, through hundreds of millions of years when it was blanketed by layers of lava, then a vast sea of sand, and then more lava until it slowly split into the present continents some 150 million years ago.

South Africa's surface has changed repeatedly, raised and lowered by subterranean upheaval, covered by sand, swamp or sea, split by volcanic rifts, weathered by climatic extremes and scoured by glaciers. The oldest form of rock, about 3.5 billion years old, and the oldest known form of life, a single-celled creature about 3.2 billion years old, have been found in Mpumalanga. The Karoo and Western Cape yield a huge variety of fossils of dinosaurs and early mammals. Some of the earliest species of mankind have been discovered in the Northern and North West provinces.

The geological contortions endowed the country with its legendary wealth in gold, diamonds, platinum and other minerals, and with its richly varied scenery –

FACING Over thousands of years the Blyde ("joyous") River has carved the third largest gorge in the world – 700m (2,310ft) deep and 57km (36 miles) long – through the Drakensberg Escarpment in Mpumalanga down to the Lowveld ("low country").

beaches, bays and lagoons along the 3,000 km (1,875 mile) coastline, mountains of many shapes and sizes, tropical plains, forests, savannah and deserts, supporting an unparalleled diversity of fauna and flora. Most of South Africa is an inland plateau dipping gradually to the desert on the west coast and sharply down the Drakensberg ("Dragon Mountains") Escarpment to the verdant, sub-tropical east coast. The plateau terrain varies from rolling savannah, seamed and studded with ridges, to empty semi-desert and flat plains. Although more than two-thirds of the land of South Africa is arid to dry with sparse vegetation, much of it is reasonable farming country.

The climate is balmy, seldom reaching the extremes. In summer it is warm in the north, hot and humid in the east, warm and dry in the central plains, hot and dry in the low arid regions, cool along the Drakensberg Escarpment and warm along the southern coast. Winter is brief, cold at night and sunny in most areas during the day. Average sunshine is about nine hours a day. Stretching from the Limpopo River in the north to Cape Agulhas in the south, and from the stark Atlantic coast in the west to the lush seaboard of the Indian Ocean in the east, the landscape of South Africa is as diverse as that in any country in the world – it is a world in one country.

ABOVE A mingerhout tree pushes its roots down through fine cracks in the rock to reach a dried-up stream bed. These trees grow to a great size and were once favoured for making wagon wheel spokes.

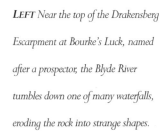

LEFT Near the top of the Drakensberg Escarpment at Bourke's Luck, named after a prospector, the Blyde River tumbles down one of many waterfalls, eroding the rock into strange shapes.

LEFT In winter the flat, empty Highveld ("high country"), lying between 1,500 and 2,500m (5,000 and 8,000ft) above sea level, becomes parched and yellow and very cold. This scene is near Wakkerstroom in Mpumalanga.

ABOVE On a rocky outcrop near Middelberg in Mpumalanga a protea bush holds its drying flowers aloft over a winter-flowering aloe and, at bottom left, the fronds of a small tree fern. These plants are typical of the Highveld vegetation.

ABOVE God's Window, on the edge of the Drakensberg Escarpment near Graskop in Mpumalanga, is so called because from 1,000m (3,300ft) above the Lowveld it gives an almost infinite view. In many places the drop from the Escarpment is vertical.

LEFT Bridal Veil Falls, near the attractive forestry town of Sabie, is one of scores of waterfalls in the Drakensberg Escarpment, some reachable only along hiking trails, others close to main roads.

BELOW Although the Free State province consists mainly of vast, almost empty sweeps of savannah, its combination of crisp clear air, mist, cloud and brilliant sunrises and sunsets creates spectacular vistas.

LEFT In the east of South Africa the sub-tropical warmth and moisture from the Indian Ocean nurture thick forests in the hills and plains traversed by many rivers, like the Hluhluwe here, flowing through northern KwaZulu/Natal.

BELOW The 374 square kilometre (144 square mile) Gariep Lake was created in the Free State by damming the Orange River to help meet the country's water and electricity needs. It is now a leading inland water resort.

LEFT This view from near the top of the Sehazini Valley, KwaZulu/Natal, gives some idea of the immense expanse of mountain scenery below the Drakensberg.

BELOW The Midmar Dam near Howick in KwaZulu/Natal is a popular yachting venue. There are more yachts on South Africa's inland lakes and dams than along its coasts.

ABOVE Few scenes any-where surpass the majesty of the Drakensberg Escarpment. In the Royal Natal National Park a resort huddles in the timbered valley below the aptly named Amphitheatre, which rises to over 3,000m (10,000ft) above sea level.

LEFT The sun rises over Sheffield Beach north of Durban. Along most of the KwaZulu/Natal coast the land and dunes are covered by exuberant tropical or sub-tropical vegetation almost to the high-water mark.

RIGHT Dramatic thunderstorms with sheet lightning and vertical strikes, like this one, are common throughout South Africa, except in the Western Cape.

ABOVE In the splendid Giant's Castle game reserve near Estcourt in KwaZulu/Natal are three great buttresses rising to over 3,000m (10,000ft) above sea level. Known as the Injasuti Triplets, two of them are visible here, under snow.

ABOVE The 360 square kilometre (139 square mile) Lake St Lucia, a shallow and complex estuary and lagoon system in northern KwaZulu/Natal, is one of the world's major wetlands, home to hundreds of thousands of animals, from elephants to sea turtles.

LEFT Zulu villages surrounded by their fields dot the ridges and slopes of KwaZulu/Natal's beautiful Valley of a Thousand Hills, so named when white settlers gave up counting the number of hills.

RIGHT In the Northern Cape the Orange River plunges deafeningly for almost 100m (330ft) into the massive, brooding canyon, 15km (9 miles) long, that it has cut through flat semi-desert.

ABOVE The Augrabies Falls are a series of 19 waterfalls which, when the Orange River is in full flood, become one of the world's six largest waterfalls.

BELOW Roads in the Augrabies National Park enable visitors to see the rare and endangered black rhino, some of which have been translocated here for safety.

RIGHT The long, narrow and barren gorge downstream from the Augrabies Falls has claimed many lives. Legend has it that the river bed is full of diamonds.

ABOVE (TOP) *The sun highlights feathery reeds and water lily leaves in a Western Cape pond.*

ABOVE (BOTTOM) *The Ceres district, a major fruit-growing area in the Western Cape, hibernates under winter snow.*

ABOVE *The cold waters of the Atlantic's Benguela Current lap 17-Mile Beach near Saldanha Bay.*

FACING *Acacia trees break up the horizon of the vast Kalahari plains.*

RIGHT *The eastern side of False Bay, lying between the Cape Peninsula and the mainland, is edged by the rugged cliffs of the Koeëlberg ("Bullet Mountains").*

ABOVE *Pringle Bay, a holiday resort at the eastern end of False Bay in the Western Cape, is dwarfed by its guardian mountains. The water is warm and the bay is famed for rock lobsters.*

LEFT *Old Cape Town suburbs sprawl on the lower slopes of Table Mountain. In the fore-ground are some of the Cape Peninsula's many thousand flower species.*

BELOW *A small gabled house lies beneath the Western Cape's Helderberg ("Bright Mountains"). The nature reserve here contains magnifi-cent flower species, mainly disa and protea, and birdlife.*

RIGHT *Yachts from around the world drop anchor in lovely Hout ("Wood") Bay and other small harbours near Cape Town. The city is known as "The Tavern of the Seas".*

RIGHT Lying north of Cape Town is the Hex River Valley, gateway between the green Cape lowlands and the semi-arid Karoo. Crammed with vineyards, the valley produces most of South Africa's export grapes.

LEFT Cape Town's old harbour has been converted into the Victoria and Alfred Waterfront, many of the old warehouses, quays and office blocks superbly restored as hotels, pubs, shops, museums, art and craft markets, and an oceanarium.

ABOVE *A highway cuts across the gently rolling hills and golden wheat-fields around Caledon in the Western Cape, renowned for its wild flower gardens on land given by Queen Victoria.*

RIGHT *This gracious old Cape Dutch farmhouse, with gabled front and end walls and wooden window shutters, is typical of farmhouses in the Western Cape winelands, the style well adapted to the Cape's hot summers and damp winters.*

LEFT *The countryside around Oudtshoorn in the Little Karoo is dry, mainly because of the rain-stopping barrier of the Outeniqua Mountains, seen here in the background. It is, however, excellent ostrich-farming country.*

FACING *The Wolfberg ("Wolf Mountain") Arch is one of many bizarre rock formations in the Cedarberg range on the West Coast. The range is popular among rock climbers and hikers and has many species of wild flowers.*

ABOVE *The cathedral-like caverns of the Cango Caves near Oudtshoorn were created over millions of years by lime-rich water filtering through the Groot Swartberg ("Big Black Mountains").*

RIGHT *Powerful waves lap the coastline in Goukama Nature Reserve. Gericke Point can be picked out in the distance.*

ABOVE *The cedars that once covered most of today's Cedarberg Wilderness Area, inland from the Cape West Coast, were felled centuries ago but the open landscape is rich in flora, including several unique species, and small wild animals.*

ABOVE *The popular Otter Trail takes hikers along the southern edge of Africa through the Tsitsikamma Coastal Park, with its dense forest and deep gorges. Marine life is protected for 5km (3 miles) from the shoreline.*

LEFT *The wild and remote Transkei coast in the Eastern Cape has dozens of small holiday resorts and chalets scattered along it, many of them at river estuaries, like these thatched homes near Mbisa.*

ABOVE (RIGHT)

Beautiful cameo scenes like this waterfall, tumbling towards the Indian Ocean, abound along the Transkei coast, a visual feast of mountains, rivers, gorges, beaches and ocean.

RIGHT Local Xhosa people call this arch "the place of sound" because of the roar of the waves crashing through it. Formed by the sea eroding a wall of offshore rock, it is the most photo-graphed phenomenon on the Transkei coast.

2

INDUSTRY & AGRICULTURE

BUILT ON DIAMONDS AND GOLD over a century ago, South Africa's economy has expanded rapidly into a complex of mining, manufacturing and service industries of First World levels. Industrial output accounts for nearly half of Africa's total industrial output. In 2004, the gross domestic product (GDP) was R927 billion (about £80 billion or US$147 billion), of which almost 40 per cent came from Gauteng province, the economic hub of the country. The national economic growth rate is about three per cent.

Manufacturing holds first place in the economy. It employs about 21 per cent of the workforce and covers an extensive range of goods, including rubber and petrol from coal, chemicals, mining and other machinery, cars, ships, clothing, most kinds of foods, weapons, timber and newsprint. South Africa exports worldwide, with machinery and motor vehicles topping the list.

Financial, insurance, real estate and business services take second place. Mining, in which about 600,000 people are employed, is third, producing mainly gold,

FACING These glossy ripe nectarines packed in straw are ready for the shelf. South Africa produces about R2.6 billion worth of fruit annually, most of it for export.

diamonds, iron ore, copper, chrome, manganese, platinum and coal. Gold is still the biggest single foreign exchange earner.

Agriculture employs about 1.2 million people and accounts for about four per cent of the GDP. South Africa produces much the same range of livestock and crops as Britain and North America but because the climate is mostly dry and fluctuates considerably, it imports some basics, such as maize and wheat periodically and beef and mutton regularly. It is a long-established exporter of wines and of citrus and other sub-tropical and deciduous fruits.

Underpinning South Africa's economy is a highly sophisticated infrastructure: over 22,000 km (13,600 miles) of railway and 73,000 km (43,000 miles) of paved roads; national and private airlines carrying more than five million people a year internally and abroad; nine main ports; annual freight traffic of some 800 million tonnes; a state-of-the-art system of almost five million fixed and almost 17 million cellular

FACING Always cold and often snow-covered in winter, but hot in summer, Prince Alfred Hamlet in the Western Cape is perfect peach-growing country, as these trees in spring blossom demonstrate.

RIGHT Tomatoes, potatoes, avocados, mangoes, onions, papayas, macadamia nuts, pineapples, pumpkins — these are just some of the fruits and vegetables produced in the fertile Lowveld of Mpumalanga.

LEFT Extremely hot and dry, but with abundant water from the Orange River, the Upington region in the Northern Cape is perfect for growing sultana grapes for sale as fresh produce or for drying.

FACING Windpumps and reservoirs are essential for survival in the Northern Cape's sheep-farming Namaqualand, where the meagre rainfall is barely enough to trigger the annual display of wild flowers.

RIGHT Because it is so hot, the region where the Kalahari intrudes into the Northern Cape has few pests, making it suitable for cotton cultivation.

telephones; nationwide electronic banking; 17 daily, 12 weekly and dozens of local newspapers and scores of magazines; and an electricity output of nearly 200,000 GWh — 65 per cent of Africa's total output. There are almost seven million motor vehicles in South Africa, half of the total number in Africa.

Some 16.3 million people (38 per cent of the population) are economically active. This is a slightly misleading statistic, however, because millions of South Africans still live traditional lives at subsistence level. The country is now focusing its resources on their advancement and that of its neighbouring countries.

ABOVE *Malmesbury, north of Cape Town in the mountain-hemmed valleys of the Swartland ("Black Country"), lies in South Africa's wheat belt. The area has been farmed since 1743.*

LEFT *Wild flowers decorate the edges of neat canals in the Northern province where water from the Luvuvhu River irrigates citrus orchards.*

FACING *A professional sheep shearer at work in the Eastern Cape contributes to South Africa's substantial output of wool and mohair.*

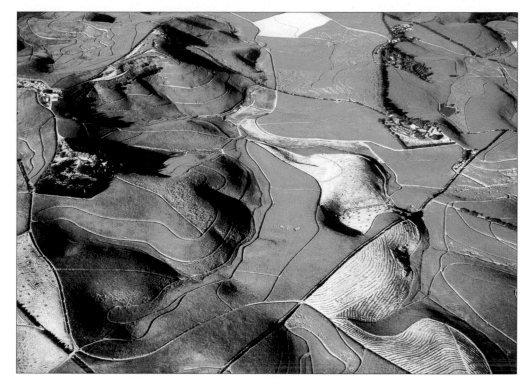

ABOVE *Seen from the air, homesteads and staff quarters are small islands in the sea of sugar cane that covers much of what were once grassy hills and forested valleys in KwaZulu/Natal.*

LEFT *A long quay was built out into Saldanha Bay on the West Coast for ore carriers to load iron ore. The ore is brought by trains that are sometimes several kilometres long.*

LEFT *Mown hay for cattle fodder is rolled into large barrel-shaped bales on a farm near Potchefstroom in Northwest province.*

LEFT *Neatly laid-out tea plantations follow the steep contours below the Drakensberg at Magoebaskloof in the Northern province.*

ABOVE To gather waterblommetjies ("little water flowers"), an essential ingredient of some traditional South African dishes, harvesters have to work waist-deep in water.

ABOVE Fishing families at Arniston on the south-ernmost tip of Africa have lived for generations in these simple, comfortable Cape Dutch homes.

RIGHT The fierce but easily caught and delectable fish species, snoek, is sold by roadside hawkers throughout the Cape Peninsula.

ABOVE Timber production is important to South Africa's economy, and the country's plantations are among the largest in the world.

ABOVE *Autumn paints the vine leaves before they fall for the winter in the Western Cape's Hex River Valley, where the hot summers yield heavy crops of table grapes for export.*

LEFT *A fat bunch of grapes, glistening with dew, is ready for picking to grace a table in some far corner of the world.*

ABOVE *The vineyards on the Hamilton Russel estate near Hermanus, east of Cape Town, are the source of some of the finest of South Africa's great variety of wines.*

ABOVE Huge old engraved vats of imported oak line the cellars of the KWV, South Africa's leading wine-making cooperative, at its headquarters in Paarl, Western Cape.

LEFT These small maturation vats are in the cellars of the Hamilton Russel estate, near Cape Town. The estate is renowned for the high quality of its Pinot Noir and Chardonnay wines.

RIGHT This view of the Hex River Valley table grape region shows typically whitewashed farm buildings lying between vineyards of Barlinka grapes.

ABOVE Miners push a heavy trolley in the sweltering heat of a gold mine tunnel, deep underground, where the ceiling has been strengthened with reinforced concrete.

RIGHT Down at the rock face, the deepest place underground, a miner holds his hydraulic drill in place with practised pressure exerted by his foot.

ABOVE At an open-cast coal mine the overburden is broken by blasting before being removed to expose the seam. South Africa has enormous coal reserves.

LEFT An indication of the size of this open-cast coal mine at Witbank in Mpumalanga is provided by the bulldozer in the centre, just below the giant bucket scraper.

RIGHT The humble Methodist Church is one of four churches, now seldom used, in Pilgrim's Rest, a preserved mining town built during the gold rush of the 1870s.

RIGHT The landscape scarred by copper mining at Nababeep, in the Namaqualand Desert of the Northern Cape, is partially softened by an ebullient display of spring flowers.

FACING The headgear of an old abandoned gold mine stands rusting on the outskirts of Johannesburg. Modern headgears are square concrete columns.

BELOW Diamonds — South Africa's best friend — remain one of the country's foremost sources of wealth. Total diamond trade in 2004 was R16 billion (about £1.4 billion/US$2.6 billion), and the South African company, De Beers, controls the world diamond market.

LEFT Molten gold is poured into bars at the Rand Refinery, which serves South Africa's gold industry. Gold exports in 2003 earned R33.1 billion (about £2.8 billion/US$5.2 billion).

LEFT At the Santarama Miniland in Johannesburg is a small-scale model of early gold mining, before the reef went too deep for open workings and new techniques had to be developed.

LEFT Zulu miners perform a traditional dance in the reconstructed part of old Johannesburg in Gold Reef City, the site of the former Crown Mine, among the richest gold mines in history.

RIGHT Visitors to Gold Reef City stroll down the street of a typical early mining village, with a headgear in the background.

RIGHT The reconstruction in Gold Reef City includes horse-drawn carriages, a hotel with "brookie lace" ironwork and many other old buildings in the classic early 20th-century style.

ABOVE Since the end of apartheid, South Africa's tourist industry has flourished. Among the major attractions are luxury game reserve lodges, such as the Sabi Sabi in the Kruger National Park.

LEFT Mala Mala, like all luxury game reserve lodges in South Africa, offers its guests the chance to see wild animals at close quarters, in this instance a herd of phlegmatic buffalo.

RIGHT Hunting game birds is a big attraction for tourists, who can hire dogs such as this golden retriever to help in hunting guinea fowl.

ABOVE During sunset game-watching drives in private reserves, tourists can view wild animals from the roofs of specially designed vehicles.

ABOVE At the Scratch Patch in Simon's Town, Cape Peninsula, customers can choose for themselves from a huge variety of polished semi-precious and plain stones.

RIGHT One of the biggest selling items in modern South Africa is the colourful South African flag, displayed on everything from flagpoles to socks.

3

WILDLIFE

S OUTH AFRICA'S HUGE AND PRECIOUS collection of wildlife is unmatched anywhere in the world. Other African states may have more of certain species, and some still experience the great wildlife migrations no longer seen in South Africa, but after the extinction of the quagga and the blue buck, the decimation of many species by hunters and the massive depredation of the sparse forests, the country's conservationists took steps to protect their valuable heritage and their efforts have paid off handsomely.

There are now 20 land and marine national parks in South Africa and about 70 provincial reserves. In addition, game abounds on hundreds of farms, some where the animals are commercially farmed, others where they are kept for tourism purposes or simply for the owners' satisfaction. More than six per cent of the land has been set aside as public reserves.

Mammals number 338 species, including southern right whales and dolphins. All of Africa's "Big Five" are here — elephant, rhino, lion, buffalo and leopard. South Africa is the only African country where both black and white rhino are adequately

FACING Cape buffalo, big cousins of domestic cattle, gather in herds

several hundred strong, sometimes thousands. These buffalo drinking in

the Sabi River are part of a much larger herd concealed by the bush.

protected and thriving. Its deserts are home to exotic antelope such as gemsbuck and springbuck. It has cheetah, hyena, wild dogs, elephant shrews, several kinds of mongoose, seals, badgers…the list is almost endless and includes a wealth of bizarre creatures such as earthworms measuring over 2m (6ft 6in) long.

Reptile species number about 400, including the largest variety of tortoises in the world and many beautiful snakes, most of them harmless.

There are nearly 900 species of birds. Different birds require different habitats and there is no one area where all species can be found. Some regions have great variety and concentrations. About 490 species have been recorded in the Kruger National Park, for example, and the parks and reserves in KwaZulu/Natal are used by a great range of sea and land birds. Vast numbers of water birds congregate in the lagoons and estuaries along the West Coast. Many species migrate from as far afield as Siberia. Many birds are highly specialized, like the heron that fishes with bait, the weaver that builds grassy apartment blocks, the vulture that likes palm nuts and the tiny penduline tit that enters its nest via a secret door.

The 80,000 or so recorded species of insect are adapted to exploit almost any environment – inside animals and man, in the sea, in rivers, in the soil, on plants and on carrion. Some insects, such as bees, flies, butterflies, weevils, moths, wasps and fleas, have been exhaustively studied. About others, such as the curious stick insects, little is known. Some, like ticks, are a nuisance and are economically harmful. Most dangerous by far is the tiny, malaria-carrying *Anopheles* mosquito. Other insects are beneficial, like the praying mantis which eats mosquitoes. Some, such as the mopane worm, are African delicacies.

In general, the people of South Africa co-exist comfortably with all these creatures. Bushpigs, baboons, leopards, snakes, wasps, spiders, scorpions and other potentially dangerous creatures are commonplace on farms and in some urban areas, but encounters are infrequent and injuries rare.

ABOVE A hippo surges from the water in a threatening display of power. The gigantic mouth is equipped with thick canines up to 60cm (2ft) long which can do terrible damage.

BELOW Buffalo can weigh up to a ton and are usually placid animals but, when angry, can become formidable opponents. Their heavy horns are respected even by lions.

BELOW *Springbok rams joust for dominance in the Kalahari Desert. Usually, jousting is in play but when they are competing for females the fighting can be fierce.*

ABOVE *Wildebeest need to drink often but they are so fearful of crocodiles that at the slightest hint of danger they flee from the water, like these wildebeest in a Mpumalanga game reserve.*

RIGHT *The suricate, a member of the mongoose family, lives in desert regions and is much photographed because of its human-like posture. These two are on sentry duty in the Kalahari.*

RIGHT *The magnificent leopard is the most wily and powerful of the big cats, a killing machine when on the hunt. It is quite common in South Africa but is seldom seen outside game reserves.*

BELOW *The white rhino is larger and heavier than the black rhino, and is clearly distinguished by its broad flat mouth. The black rhino has a prehensile lip and is a browser.*

FACING A creature of the night, the thick-tailed bushbaby (or galago) is often seen in camps in eastern game reserves. The big eyes help it hunt insects in the dark.

LEFT An opportunistic black-backed jackal lurks among a springbuck herd drinking in the Kalahari Gemsbok National Park in the hope of finding a stray calf.

FACING The honey-badger (or ratel), an omnivorous and nocturnal animal, supplements its diet by raiding bee hives, hence its name. It is apparently immune to bee stings.

RIGHT Africa's wild horse and one of the main items in the diets of lions, leopards, hyenas and other predators, the skittish zebra has only its speed for defence.

ABOVE A young cheetah scans the sunny grasslands of KwaZulu/Natal for prey. Cheetahs are the fastest animals on four legs.

LEFT Because their skins are very sensitive to the sun, hippos spend most of the day in the water. Here, hippos in KwaZulu/Natal's Mkuzi game reserve provide a perch for a cattle egret.

RIGHT The delicate Cape fox is not often seen because it lives in deserts, such as the Kalahari, where it feeds mainly on mice and insects.

LEFT *A giraffe less than a year old stares inquisitively at the photographer from the reassurance of its mother's side in the Mala Mala private game reserve.*

ABOVE *Cuddly looking hyena cubs, still too innocent to be cautious, sunbathe near the entrance to their burrow. Female hyenas are fiercely protective of their young.*

BELOW *Safety for a baby elephant is the massive bulk of its mother and the presence of the rest of the herd. Youngsters are sometimes attacked by lions.*

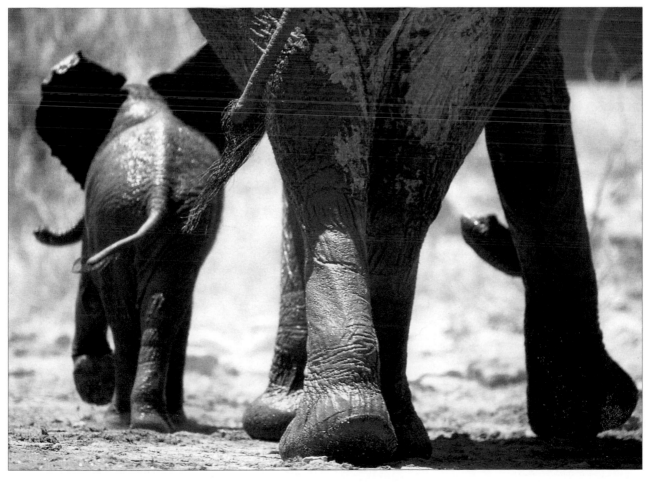

LEFT *The waterbuck, seen here in KwaZulu/Natal's Hluhluwe Park, is so named because it favours rivers and wetlands. It is the only buck with a ring on its rump.*

BOTTOM (LEFT) *These wild dog pups, sitting at the entrance to their lair, will develop coat patterns that are as distinctive as fingerprints.*

BOTTOM (RIGHT) *Crocodiles are outstanding mothers and gently carry their newly hatched young from nest to water in their powerful jaws and in the pouch beneath the jaws.*

LEFT *A heavy-maned male lion lazily roars his announcement that the evening's hunting is about to begin, displaying the fangs that all animals in Africa respect.*

BOTTOM (LEFT) *A family of dwarf mongooses sunbathes on a termite heap. Incurably inquisitive, dwarf mongooses vanish instantly when approached but generally re-emerge within minutes.*

BOTTOM (RIGHT) *Nocturnal but often seen by day in the Kgalagadi Transfrontier Park, the quill-armoured porcupine is Africa's largest rodent.*

ABOVE The classic
African scene – a solitary
bull elephant strolls in
majestic splendour
beneath a stormy sky,
master of all he surveys.

RIGHT Wild dogs, an
endangered species, have
an extremely close-knit
family system and take
great care of their pups.

ABOVE Dust rises as the
two-ton bodies of these
white rhino bulls collide in
a territorial dispute in the
Kruger National Park.
Sometimes such fights
are fatal.

RIGHT A grey vervet monkey eats the blossoms of a flame creeper in the Kruger National Park. Very common in the subtropics, these monkeys have become a pest in some areas.

LEFT South Africa is famous for its many species of tortoise. This magnificent beast is commonly known as the leopard or mountain tortoise.

RIGHT Warthogs are plentiful in South Africa's northern and eastern regions. In spite of their razor-sharp teeth, they are delectable to many predators.

LEFT In their play with "toys" such as tree branches and with each other, lion cubs learn many of the skills they will need to survive when they become adults.

BELOW Gemsbok bulls battle over territory in the Kgalagadi Transfrontier Park. Their strength, speed and lance-like horns make them one of the most feared of antelope, respected even by lions.

RIGHT The dainty klipspringer, seen here in the Kruger National Park, is about 60cm (2ft) high at the shoulder and has hooves specially adapted to its rocky habitats. The hairs of its coat are hollow, for warmth.

ABOVE *Sunrise in the Kruger National Park silhouettes a giraffe and trees on the still water of a pond — a typical scene in the many game reserves in the Lowveld.*

LEFT *A superb example of the rather scarce sable antelope, this powerful bull in the Lowveld displays perfectly matched horns. The oxpeckers clinging to his hide feed on ticks and other parasites.*

LEFT Giant girdled lizards, reaching 30cm (1ft) long and looking like small dinosaurs, live in colonies dug into the sand in central South Africa. They are also known as sungazers because they like to bask in the sun.

BELOW The Cape ground squirrel is an inhabitant of the desert. It lives in colonies in warrens dug into the sand, emerging cautiously to forage.

LEFT A female fruit bat with her offspring clinging to her belly hangs by her claws from the roof of a cave. These bats have fox-like faces and feed by night.

LEFT *Only the head of this waterbuck is visible above tall grass in the Kruger National Park but it is immediately identifiable by its curved, slightly forward-swept horns.*

BELOW *Many people rate the greater kudu as the most beautiful of all buck, with its gracefully spiralled horns, attractive markings and elegant stride. It can easily clear a 2m (6ft 6in) fence from a standing jump.*

LEFT For the first few months of their lives baby baboons spend most of their time riding on their mothers' backs or clinging to their bellies. Baboons take excellent care of their young.

BELOW Cape buffalo come down past a grazing impala to drink at a waterhole. These animals can go for quite long periods without water if the grazing is good.

RIGHT Pound for pound, the toughest animal in Africa is the honey-badger (or ratel), whose power, thick hide, sharp claws and irascibility have been known to make even a lion think twice.

ABOVE *Their glossy coats showing that they are in good health, an impala ewe is nuzzled by her lamb in the Kruger National Park, where they out-number all other buck and are the main prey of the larger predators.*

LEFT *The big ears of a kudu cow can pick up the sounds of danger from a considerable distance away. Like this one, they tend to be inquisitive animals.*

ABOVE *Lesser flamingos are found in many parts of South Africa, wherever there are stretches of water containing enough of the microscopic algae and plankton they filter out with their inverted beaks.*

LEFT *The brown-hooded kingfisher, unlike most of the nine other kingfisher species in South Africa, hunts mainly on dry land for anything from scorpions and crickets to lizards, mice and small snakes.*

RIGHT One of South Africa's most spectacular birds is the crimson-breasted shrike, whose flame-red chest is clearly visible in its arid western habitat.

BELOW The orange-breasted bush shrike, with its striking sunburst plumage, inhabits the warmer, wetter northern and eastern areas of the country.

RIGHT The African marsh harrier is so called because it commonly flies low over wetlands as it hunts for frogs, small rodents, nestlings and similar prey.

ABOVE A pied kingfisher sits on a perch with its catch in the Kruger National Park. It will deftly juggle the fish around in its beak until it is in the right position, then quickly swallow it head first.

ABOVE The white-backed vulture, whose wingspan exceeds 2m (6ft 6in), is common right across the north of South Africa, from desert to tropics. This one is perched in a tree in the Kgalagadi Transfrontier Park.

LEFT One of the comics of the Kruger National Park, with its lumbering flight and wobbly landings, is the yellow-billed hornbill. This one is eating insects in the park's Satara camp.

LEFT The markings and plumage of this white-faced owl give it excellent camouflage on its nest in a camelthorn tree in the Northern province. These owls hunt mainly rodents and other birds.

LEFT The garishly coloured, goose-sized ground hornbill is one of South Africa's larger birds, often seen walking around in game reserves. A voracious feeder, it swallows small mammals and reptiles whole, including hares and live snakes.

LEFT This young martial eagle will develop into one of the largest and most awesome raptors. They kill prey not with their beaks but with their sharp, powerful claws.

ABOVE A blacksmith plover bathes in a rain puddle. Its name derives from its routine call, which is like the distant sound of a hammer striking an anvil.

RIGHT Young collared sunbirds wait expectantly to be fed by their hard-working parents, who look after them for a month or more after birth.

RIGHT A white pelican comes in for a landing in KwaZulu/Natal's Mkuzi game reserve, while the flock lines up on the water to hunt fish together.

BELOW In South Africa the crested guinea fowl is found only in the north-eastern sub-tropical terrain, such as that in the Kruger National Park. They feed on a wide variety of items, from berries to beetles.

LEFT The nectar of proteas is part of the diet of the Cape sugarbird, found in the far south between the West Coast and Port Elizabeth. Other items include spiders and insects.

BELOW The black-headed oriole, with its vividly contrasting colours, is one of the more striking residents of the Lowveld and its clear song is usually heard before the bird is seen.

LEFT The South African or "jackass" penguin, named for its harsh call, occurs only on the South African coast and islands. Once found in large numbers, the population has been greatly reduced by overfishing and by oil pollution from ships.

RIGHT Few birds have plumage as brightly coloured as that of the Knysna lourie. About as big as a bantam, this species inhabits the forests along the warm east coast.

FAR RIGHT The ubiquitous ostrich, largest of all birds, brought fortunes to farmers at the turn of the century when its feathers were highly fashionable. It is now becoming popular for its meat and hide.

RIGHT The crowned crane, found only in the north-east of the country, becomes quite tame but is a bad-tempered bird likely to bite the hand that feeds it.

ABOVE *The iridescent blue on this plum-coloured starling glistens in the sunlight. These birds feed mainly on fruit and are seasonal migrants to the northern regions of South Africa.*

LEFT *The imperious expression and golden eye of the martial eagle, a bird large enough to kill small buck, show why royalty through the ages have chosen eagles as a symbol of power.*

LEFT Dragonflies are one of the more aggressive predators in the teeming world of insects, snatching other insects in flight, including other dragonflies.

RIGHT A member of the large family of short-horned grasshoppers feeds on a juicy bud. Most of these grasshoppers are fairly harmless but some can do great damage to gardens and crops.

BELOW Like some monster from outer space, a hairy but harmless luna moth displays its huge antennae, shaped like fern fronds.

ABOVE *The harmless damselfly is similar to, but not to be confused with, the predatory dragonfly. Clouds of damselflies sometimes appear in South Africa's tropical and sub-tropical forests.*

RIGHT *A single-horned praying mantis waits motionless to snatch an insect. Many mantises are camouflaged to resemble the plants in which they hunt.*

BELOW *An African honeybee, covered in pollen, gathers nectar. This species was introduced into South America where it has since become a menace.*

ABOVE The termites that built this tower in the Limpopo Province may have tunnelled hundreds of metres down to find water. Each of the several species of termites in South Africa has a specialized diet and a complex social structure.

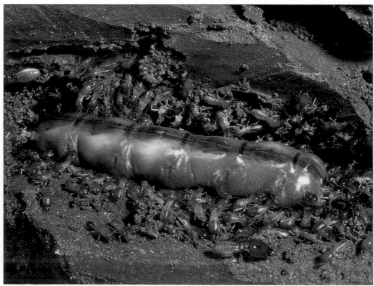

LEFT A termite queen does nothing but eat and lay eggs while the workers attend her constantly and the soldiers, with their big red armoured heads, protect her.

LEFT Without the energetic dung beetle, it is said, Africa would be covered in animal droppings. Dung beetles have been exported to Australia to save it from being buried in cattle dung.

BELOW Dung beetles (or scarabs) bury an elephant dropping in the Addo National Park. They feed on dung and make balls from it in which to lay their eggs.

ABOVE A mass of recently hatched ladybird (ladybug) beetles mill about before taking off to begin life elsewhere. They are useful to gardeners in destroying some parasites.

LEFT The red velvet mite, resembling a tiny cushion, belongs to the same family as spiders. It is one of many species of African mites, some harmful, others not, that live on animals and plants.

LEFT *Sea anemones filter the currents with their red tentacles in the Western Cape tidal zone. These sea creatures come in many colours.*

ABOVE *This unusual shell is found only at Plettenberg Bay, renowned for the great variety of shells washed up on its beaches.*

BELOW (LEFT) *Sea stars move slowly across an algae-encrusted rock in shallow water on the Western Cape coast.*

BELOW (RIGHT) *An exceptionally attractive sea anemone extends its white-tipped tentacles to attract prey.*

ABOVE A sea urchin, whose spines can inflict painful wounds on anyone who steps on them, shares a tidal pool in the Western Cape with an unusually bright starfish.

LEFT A forest of coral polyps waves gently in the currents sweeping across a coral reef in the tropical Indian Ocean off the northern shore of KwaZulu/Natal.

4

FLORA

Within the borders of South Africa is the greatest concentration and variety of flowers in the world. This floral heritage, discovered more than three centuries ago, continues to excite botanists and has given the world a host of well-known garden species, such as agapanthus, Barberton daisy and gladiolus.

The known number of plant species in the country currently stands at about 23,000, with new species still being found. Almost every province boasts a wide range of plant life, from giant trees to many types of orchids. The huge diversity of species in the Western Cape — nearly 9,000 — is such that the province has been declared one of the world's six "floral kingdoms". Cape Town's Table Mountain alone has some 1,500 indigenous species, more than the number in the whole of Britain. A region which may hold a similar profusion of plant life was recently identified in the sub-tropical area in the north of the Kruger National Park.

FACING Like gold in a pirate's treasure chest, Grielum humifusum,

a member of the rose family, spreads its buttercup yellow flowers in the

sunshine during Namaqualand's annual pageant of wild flowers.

One of the greatest floral spectacles in the world, visited every year by growing numbers of South Africans and foreigners, occurs in the unlikeliest place – the usually bleak and dry Namaqualand Desert along the Northern Cape coast. Spring rains in Namaqualand sometimes fail and are sparse at best, but when they do come the flowers seize the opportunity. For several weeks the entire landscape, as far as the eye can see in every direction, is carpeted with a kaleidoscope of the colours of billions of wild flowers, their perfume filling the air.

The Kirstenbosch Gardens, established in 1913 and lying on the south side of Table Mountain, are almost as famous as London's Kew Gardens for their floral wealth and for the contribution they have made to botany. They cover nearly 6 square kilometres (about 2.5 square miles) but only about six per cent of the area is cultivated; this part alone has 6,000 species of indigenous plants, and the herbarium holds more than 250,000 species.

Other, smaller botanical gardens are scattered around the country, each focusing mainly on local plant life. The one at Nelspruit in Mpumalanga is second only to Kirstenbosch, with a wonderful array of sub-tropical and tropical trees, orchids, shrubs, creepers and other greenery.

In the far north of South Africa the landscape is dominated by baobabs, some of them possibly 4,000 years old. In the far south the yellowwoods, many of them 1,000 years old, tower above humid jungle festooned with creepers. Between these extremes is an almost infinite variety of plant life, from armies of aloes and the curious quiver trees to brilliant bauhinnias, succulent plants in many shapes and sizes, and the hallmark of Africa, the familiar thorn trees.

ABOVE AND RIGHT *Seedlings of the Australian "wonder tree" have been imported in an attempt to prevent indigenous trees from being used by rural dwellers for firewood. The tree grows so fast it is said that a backyard patch of 50 to 60 trees can keep a family adequately supplied with firewood and livestock fodder.*

LEFT AND BELOW The long-stalked Aloe ferox *is a substitute for confectionery for many rural African children, who suck the nectar from its red blossoms. Common in the Western Cape, it is one source of a medicinal gel widely used in cosmetics and is an important winter food for sunbirds.*

RIGHT The lovely Outeniqua heather, Erica versicolor, grows in the Western Cape's prolific "floral kingdom", where throughout the year flowers of one kind or another are in bloom.

BELOW These distinctive pincushion proteas, Leucospermum cordifolius, grow in the reserve on the Helderberg, near the town of Somerset West in the Western Cape.

LEFT Impala lilies on their fat grey stems are a striking feature of the Lowveld in Mpumalanga and the Limpopo Province, especially in dry periods when the land is otherwise bare.

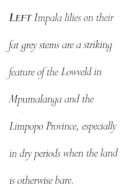

LEFT A typical Western Cape scene — cultivated roses and lawns surround an old Cape Dutch home beneath the Helderberg in the heart of South Africa's wine-making region.

LEFT Blue wild flowers and green lichen grow in the depths of the Blyde River canyon in Mpumalanga. The gorge, third largest in the world, hosts a wide range of plants, from tropical to temperate species.

BELOW The silver tree, Leucadendron argenteum, *a striking member of the Proteaceae family, is unique to the Western Cape.*

ABOVE *A spring feast of drosanthemum flowers glows in the sunlight.*

LEFT The umbrella thorn, Acacia tortilis, *seen here in the Mkuzi game reserve in KwaZulu/Natal, is one of Africa's best-known trees and an important provider of shade for man and animal.*

5

PARKS & RESERVES

ALL OF SOUTH AFRICA'S 20 NATIONAL PARKS and most of the 70 or so provincial parks and reserves were created to conserve particular segments of the natural environment – a specific assemblage of wildlife, a particular ecology, certain types of animal or plants – and to give people the opportunity to enjoy the marvels of nature and learn about the need for conservation.

The renowned Kruger National Park was established to prevent the extinction of a cross-section of the exceptionally abundant and diverse animal and plant life in South Africa's Lowveld. One of the world's first national parks, created in 1898 and proclaimed in 1926, it is also one of the finest, not only for wildlife but also for the excellent amenities it offers to more than one million visitors a year.

Less well known but in fact larger and more dramatic is the Kgalagadi Transfrontier Park, extraordinary because it is a cross-border venture between South Africa and neighbouring Botswana. It teems with the animals, birds, reptiles

FACING The convoluted tangle of trunk, branches and twigs of a baobab tree, like this one in the Kruger National Park, is an environment of its own, providing food and shelter to a variety of resident creatures as well as to passing animals.

and insects peculiar to the great Kalahari Desert against a spectacular backdrop of ancient, bright red dunes and blistering white plains.

Addo/Zuurberg is in the Eastern Cape. The Addo section shelters black and white rhino and the last few hundred of the elephants that once roamed in their thousands in this area. The Zuurberg part preserves indigenous mountain vegetation such as the cushion bush and a cycad species found nowhere else in the country.

The Karoo National Park in the Western Cape conserves the delightful array of animal and plant life indigenous to a seemingly dreary landscape that travellers tend to speed through. The Marakele National Park in the Northwest province was created to protect the ecology of the great Waterberg plateau where the writer and philosopher Eugene Marais found his inspiration.

Parks in KwaZulu/Natal and the Eastern and Western

ABOVE *Sundowner time around the fire in Kruger's Bateleur camp gives visitors the chance to meet each other and exchange stories about the day's events.*

BELOW *Kruger staff pamper a baby black rhino abandoned by its mother when it got stuck in mud. When raised by people, such young animals cannot be returned to the wild and have to go to zoos.*

Cape extend out to sea to protect coral, turtles, fish, otters and other ocean and coastal life. In contrast, the Ai-Ais/Richtersveld Transfrontier Park in the Northern Cape — sun-blasted, oven-hot and mostly empty — extends over an utterly entrancing landscape of rock and naked mountains. The Golden Gate National Park in the Free State protects spectacular sandstone bluffs in mountain terrain favoured by unusual buck and birds.

Commerce, industry and individuals alike have enthusiastically entered the conservation game. A game reserve company is pioneering the use of resource reserves to benefit local communities. Two small reserves in Mpumalanga have been created by forestry companies to save the endangered blue swallow, of which fewer than a dozen nesting pairs remain. There are scores of private reserves and game farms.

South Africa is an acknowledged leader in wildlife management and research and provides conservation advice and assistance to many African countries.

ABOVE (TOP) Impala, here all lined up to drink, are the commonest buck in Kruger, numbering about 200,000 and found throughout the park. They are the prime food of many predators.

ABOVE The elephant hall at Letaba camp commemorates some of Kruger's giant tuskers, among them the "Magnificent Seven". Because they are protected, many Kruger elephants have unusually large tusks.

LEFT Although bitter, the fruit growing on the bark of the knobbly fig tree found in the hot northern parts of the Kruger National Park is eaten by animals and birds. Elephants eat the leaves.

ABOVE *The hollows in the head of this solitary bull in the Phinda resource reserve, KwaZulu/Natal, indicate that he is getting on in years. Elephants' average life-span is slightly less than man's.*

RIGHT *A big heavy-maned lion in the Phinda reserve cuddles up to a nubile young lioness, her juvenile spots still faintly visible.*

ABOVE The majestic Drakensberg Amphitheatre lies within the Royal Natal National Park, where tourist accommodation includes a hotel, chalets and campsites.

LEFT South African game experts lead the world in the capture and translocation of wild animals. This tranquillized white rhino in the Umfolozi reserve, KwaZulu/Natal, is being crated for transport.

ABOVE *Giraffe, like most animals in the Hluhluwe reserve, KwaZulu/Natal, are so accustomed to vehicles that they generally ignore them. They have right of way anyway.*

LEFT *After eating their fill, cheetah laze in the sun in a KwaZulu/Natal park. They have to feed quickly when they have killed, or hyenas might seize their prey.*

RIGHT *Burchell's zebra drinking in the Umfolozi reserve show their finely drawn face markings. The markings of no two zebra are exactly alike.*

BELOW *The Ntshondwe camp in the Itala reserve in northern KwaZulu/Natal has become one of the province's most popular camps, with its waterhole and hides and abundant wildlife.*

ABOVE *Clouds of morning mist drift over the forest and grassland of the Hluhluwe reserve before the rising sun melts them away.*

LEFT *In the Spioenkop nature reserve in KwaZulu/Natal, the Tugela River has been dammed to form a lake. Rhino and a variety of buck live in the game park.*

ABOVE *Sparring young gemsbok kick up dust in the Kgalagadi Transfrontier Park, Northern Cape, while their longer-horned elders appear to egg them on.*

LEFT *The small Skilpad wild flower reserve in the far north of the Northern Cape desert is named after the tortoises living there. All South African tortoises are protected by law.*

LEFT *Sunsets in the Kalahari produce dramatic streaks of colour across skies of startling clarity, displaying a profusion of stars when there is no moon.*

ABOVE The kokerboom (or quiver tree) is one of the few plants that grow to a significant size in the dry Northern Cape. The San people used the bark to make quivers for their arrows.

ABOVE A herd of Africa's largest antelope, the massive eland, thunders across the red sands of the Kalahari. Eland are easily domesticated and attempts have been made to farm them.

LEFT The Orange River flowing in full flood through the bleak, barren gorge, over 100m (330ft) deep, in the Augrabies National Park is an awesome spectacle.

LEFT *The thin grasses and spare scrub of the Western Cape's Karoo National Park sustain a surprisingly large variety of wildlife.*

FACING *They are flat and apparently desolate, but the great salt marshes of the West Coast National Park are full of hardy plants and small creatures which support many thousands of water and other birds.*

BELOW *The changing light and sky during the day over the Karoo, a largely featureless landscape save for the flat-topped mountains, create scenes of breathtaking beauty.*

LEFT The huge Langebaan lagoon in the West Coast National Park is part of Saldanha Bay, a favourite venue for keen sailors.

ABOVE A large colony of South African or "jackass" penguins lives in safety on Jutten Island, one of four islands in the West Coast National Park.

RIGHT The desolate Postberg section of the West Coast National Park, with its rocks sculpted into strange shapes by wind and water, comes alive in spring when the wild flowers bloom.

RIGHT The Bontebok National Park was created along the Breede ("Broad") River in the Western Cape to save the bontebok from extinction when there were only 22 of these animals left. They are now thriving in several provinces.

BELOW (LEFT) Ostrich breeding at Oudtshoorn has saved these birds from danger. One of the attractions for visitors is a ride on an ostrich, which is nearly as fast as a horse.

BELOW (RIGHT) Autumn leaves decorate the forest floor in the Wilderness National Park on the Garden Route.

RIGHT Beautiful Sandy Beach is one of many scenic pleasures on the Otter Trail, which extends 41km (25 miles) along the Garden Route coastline.

BELOW At the western end of the Otter Trail is Nature's Valley, a long white beach and lagoon on the coast of the Tsitsikamma National Park in the Western Cape.

LEFT The elephants in the Addo National Park near Port Elizabeth are descended from a few survivors of great herds that roamed the Eastern Cape before hunters moved in. Now they number several hundred.

6

CITIES & TOWNS

SOUTH AFRICA HAS A HANDFUL OF MAJOR CITIES, over 20 smaller cities and hundreds of towns, villages, hamlets and outposts, some little more than a trading store and a post office. The towns generally reflect their environments; some still have the appearance of wild, frontier settlements, others are old and quaint, a number of them gaining vigorous new life as the country's demography alters. The cities differ sharply in character, depending upon location, economic activity and predominant culture.

The largest by far is not one city but a conglomeration of cities crowding the smallest province, Gauteng. At its core is Johannesburg, which began as one of the many gold rush camps spawned by the Witwatersrand ("White Waters Ridge") gold strikes in 1885–6. Urban growth, especially recently, has been so rapid that Johannesburg, Pretoria 50km (31 miles) north, the new Midrand between them, Vereeniging to the south, Randburg, Soweto and the other municipalities are now one huge metropolis accommodating most of Gauteng's nearly 9 million people.

Scarred by mine workings, ringed by monotonous "townships", blotched with squatter camps and veined with freeways, it is an unlovely metropolis. But it has many beautiful suburbs, an extraordinary dynamism, and a vigorous arts and entertainment

FACING Hillbrow, one of the most densely populated square miles in the world, is a forest of apartment blocks on top of a hill in central Johannesburg. The tall building on the right is a cylindrical apartment block; in the middle is a broadcasting tower.

culture. The economic heart of the country, it smells of money and is never boring.

By far the loveliest city is Cape Town, the legislative capital lying in the lap of Table Mountain. Over 350 years old, it has spread around the Cape Peninsula to False Bay in the east and the Atlantic Ocean in the west, clinging between sea and cliffs. Its 3.5 million people of many races enjoy a leisurely way of life amid historic and scenic beauty. The Suez Canal has taken away most of the ocean traffic that once called in here but the city remains a fairly active port and is the headquarters for many financial institutions and industries.

Durban is South Africa's vacation capital. With its Florida-style skyscraper beachfront and big, busy harbour, it is almost as lively as Johannesburg but enjoys a euphoria generated by a steamy climate, golden beaches and a stunningly beautiful hinterland. History has given it an English personality, spiced with the cultures of India and enlivened by the Zulu people.

Pretoria, Afrikaans in personality and once a dreary administrative capital, has abruptly emerged from its bureaucratic cocoon as a vivacious, cosmopolitan city thanks to a huge injection of diplomats, money and activity since South Africa rejoined the international community. Always an architectural showcase, it is booming with new construction.

Bloemfontein is South Africa's judicial capital and carries on as placidly as ever on the distant Free State plains. Kimberley, once the hectic focus of great diamond wealth, sleeps prettily

ABOVE Johannesburgers on their way to work stroll through the small Joubert Park, below Hillbrow, in the central business district.

BELOW The flea market at Bruma Lake, an artificial waterfront in Randburg, Johannesburg, attracts swarms of traders and customers every Saturday.

LEFT The only means of transport for visitors to Gold Reef City, a reconstruction of an old mining town on the outskirts of Johannesburg, are horse-drawn carriages.

under the Northern Cape sun, dreaming of the past. East London was built to serve the 1820 settlers and now serves the Eastern Cape's large black population. Port Elizabeth is the home of South Africa's automobile industry.

With the change from four provinces to nine, new provincial capitals have emerged. Some, such as Mpumalanga's Nelspruit, North West's Mmabatho and Eastern Cape's Bisho, are not yet cities. But they are likely to grow fast. The drift of people from rural to urban centres is steady in modern South Africa.

ABOVE *The home of soccer, South Africa's most popular sport, is the huge FNB sports stadium in Johannesburg.*

RIGHT *Centurion Park cricket ground near Pretoria was built in 1985 and is a major venue for provincial and international matches.*

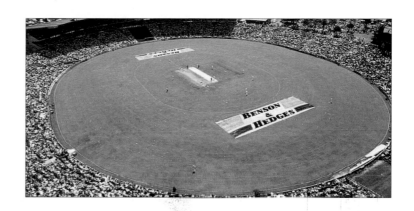

BELOW *Johannesburg's Ellis Park rugby stadium, built in 1989, is flanked by Hillbrow on the right and the downtown business area on the left.*

LEFT *This monument in Johannesburg was erected to honour the black miners who operate the rockface drills deep underground.*

RIGHT *Southgate shopping centre is one of many malls, each containing scores of shops, scattered all over Johannesburg's suburbs.*

RIGHT The clean, elegant lines of the skyscrapers in central Pretoria are silhouetted by the setting sun. In the foreground are the gardens of the Union Buildings.

BELOW Since the birth of the new South Africa, airlines from all over the world now fly into Johannesburg's international airport, located on the high altitude plains east of the city.

BELOW Pretoria lies in a valley between two mountain ridges at the eastern end of the Magaliesberg range and can be very hot in summer.

LEFT The Palace of the Lost City in the wilds of the Northwest province is a multi-million rand architectural extravaganza of African and Eastern images, housing a hotel, casino and golf complex.

LEFT Durban's beachfront is a long parade of high-rise hotels, nightclubs, pubs, bistros, restaurants and other attractions for the visitors drawn by its warm climate when the rest of the country is gripped by winter.

RIGHT Street vendors are fast taking over the sidewalks in South Africa's cities and towns but their informal trade is a key part of the economy.

FAR RIGHT Sunday trading was barred in the old South Africa but is now permitted. Here, an Indian flower seller plies his trade in Durban.

LEFT Durban's colourful stalls sell everything from key rings to curry powders rated between "mild" and "atomic", and are as great an attraction for holiday-makers as the beaches and pubs.

LEFT The glitter of central Durban at night is mirrored by the waters of the yacht basin in the harbour, a haven for sailors from all over the world.

BELOW Pietermaritzburg's city hall reflects the pleasant Victorian character of this provincial capital, despite its Afrikaans name.

RIGHT The open-air market on the lawns in front of Durban's Maharani Hotel gives the beachfront a carnival atmosphere.

BELOW The Workshop in central Durban is an old railway workshop which has been cleverly converted into a big, bustling shopping mall.

RIGHT The public swimming pools on Durban's beachfront are a children's paradise but at the height of the holiday season they vanish beneath a sea of humanity.

RIGHT *Vryburg is the centre of a large ranching and dairy farming region in the flat, dry plains of the Northwest province and boasts a modern town hall.*

ABOVE *The Lord Milner Hotel in the charming hamlet of Matjiesfontein, north of Cape Town, became a British regimental headquarters during the Anglo-Boer War and has been restored to its Victorian charm.*

RIGHT *Putsonderwater ("well with no water"), a remote railway station in the arid Northern Cape, is typical of thousands of such outposts all over the country. There is an annual contest for the most beautifully kept one.*

LEFT *This view of Cape Town shows the urban development along the northern Cape Peninsula, with Hout Bay in the foreground, the sprawling eastern suburbs and Cape Flats on the upper right and the back of the Table Mountain on the upper left.*

RIGHT *No shot has ever been fired in anger from the ramparts of the 330-year-old, Dutch-built Cape Town Castle, the oldest building in South Africa.*

RIGHT *The Strand is a pretty resort town on False Bay favoured by pensioners and holidaymakers from inland. Beyond is Gordon's Bay, another holiday resort, and beyond that rise the Hottentots Holland Mountains.*

ABOVE *In the holiday season The Strand puts on firework displays along its beachfront and from the top of nearby apartment blocks. Its beach is very safe for children.*

LEFT *The beautiful town of Montagu, Western Cape, is famed for its excellent wines, deciduous fruits, hot springs, magnificent views, indigenous flower garden and historical architecture.*

ABOVE *The Victoria and Albert Waterfront, a multi-million rand redevelopment of Cape Town's old harbour, functions as a business and residential area as well as a major tourist attraction.*

LEFT *In the heart of Cape Town is the cobbled Greenmarket Square, surrounded by beautiful old buildings and dominated by the grandeur of Table Mountain, here wearing its "tablecloth" of clouds.*

RIGHT *Jameson Hall is one of the many attractive buildings on the campus of the University of Cape Town, which lies on the mountain slope behind Devil's Peak.*

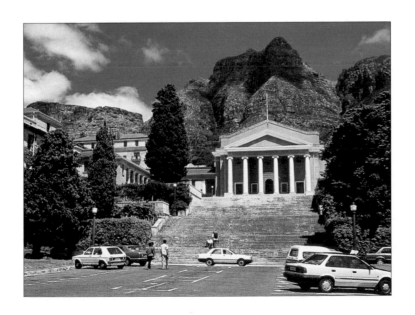

ABOVE *The War Memorial and the South African Museum stand in The Gardens in Cape Town, an area where, over three centuries ago, the Dutch grew vegetables to supply passing ships.*

ABOVE Lawns and apartment blocks fringe the coastline of suburban Port Elizabeth, the historic city founded in 1820 when English settlers landed at Algoa Bay. It is South Africa's fifth largest port.

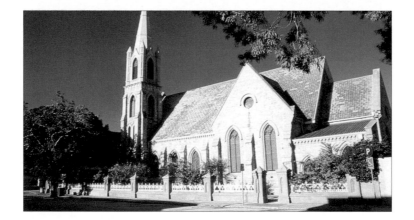

LEFT The Holy Trinity church is one of many buildings of religious and historical importance in Port Elizabeth.

RIGHT Port Elizabeth's modern central business district rises above a break-water made of a South African invention called "dolos" — interlocked six-armed concrete shapes.

RIGHT *Grahamstown is an important cultural and educational centre, the venue for Africa's leading annual arts festival, and the site of Rhodes University, founded by Cecil John Rhodes.*

BELOW *In front of the picturesque town hall in East London, South Africa's only river port, is an equestrian statue built to commemorate residents killed in the Anglo-Boer War.*

LEFT *Port Alfred, lying between Port Elizabeth and East London, was established by the 1820 English settlers and is now a popular holiday resort, with many seaside and freshwater attractions.*

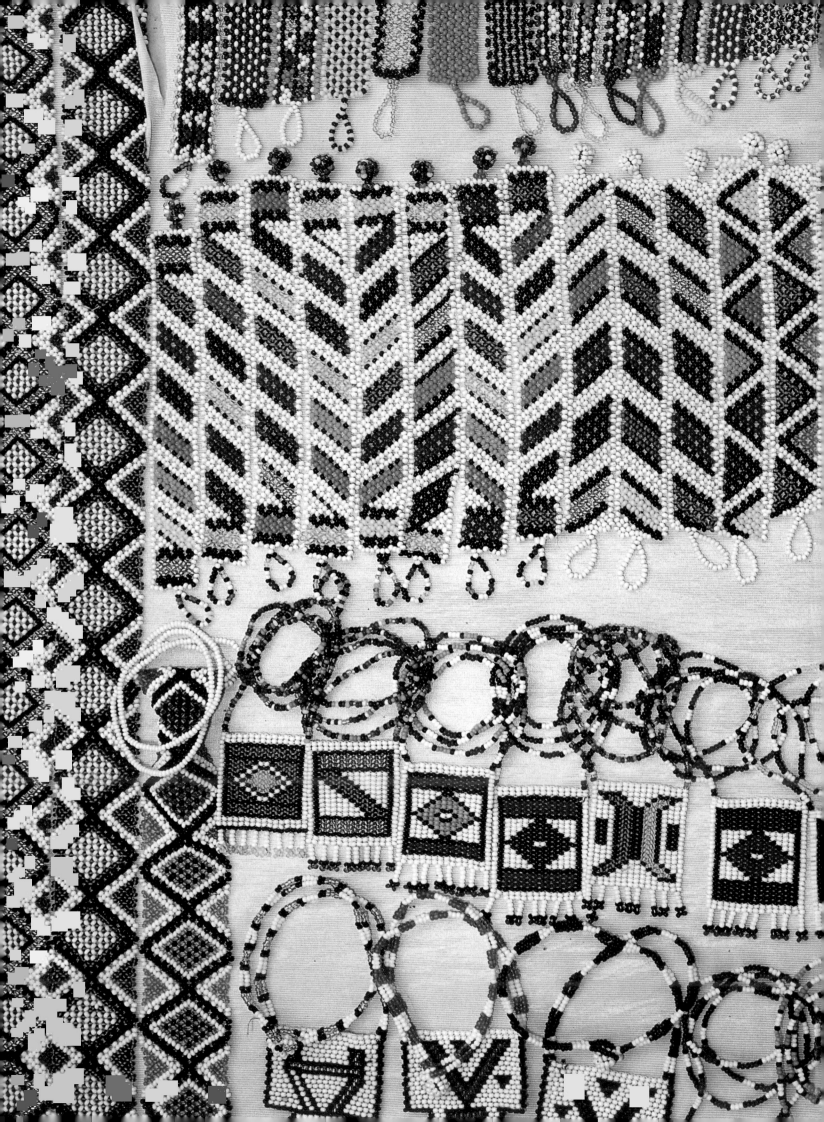

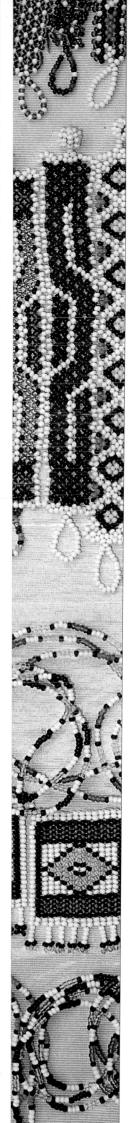

7

ARTS & CRAFTS

THE EVOLUTION OF ART is perhaps nowhere seen more clearly than in Africa, the cradle of mankind. In South Africa, long exposed to the cultures of Europe and the East, modern conventional art in all its forms thrives side by side with the art of many African cultures. These traditions influence each other powerfully. The result is an outstanding pageant of works whose quality South Africans themselves have begun to appreciate only in recent decades. Now, at last, the artists are receiving the accolades they deserve and their works are being seen outside private collections and galleries, gracing the foyers and walls of business and government buildings and being exhibited and sold abroad.

It is commonplace to see the bold designs the Ndebele people paint on their houses and the Zulus weave into their beadwork now reproduced on anything from office blocks to buses to stationery. Works by leading artists such as Sidney Kumalo, Percy Konqobe and Meshak Raphalalani, whose sculptures in wood reflect both

FACING Elaborate, traditional beadwork has more than just a decorative purpose. It plays an important part in ritual and social affairs, each colour having a meaning and the designs denoting a person's status and conveying messages, such as love letters.

8

PEOPLE
& CULTURES

SOUTHERN AFRICA WAS A GREAT STEW OF PEOPLES of different races, cultures, languages, religions and skills for centuries before Afrikaner nationalists imposed apartheid in an attempt to separate its ingredients Arabs were trading down Africa's east coast, probably as far south as the Tropic of Capricorn, before the birth of Christ, and Indian and Chinese voyagers visited southern Africa long before the first Europeans sailed round it. All left their influence and some of their blood among the black peoples.

They came for ivory and for the gold of the Monomatapa kingdom that covered most of present-day Zimbabwe and produced an estimated 25 million ounces of gold in the 12 centuries from about AD650. Further south, migrating blacks intermingled with the Khoi and San races, who spoke with the distinctive click sounds that are now a feature of the Zulu and Xhosa languages. Portuguese navigators rounded the Cape in

FACING Who knows what blood runs in the veins of this elderly woman carrying firewood to her home in the Western Cape? Certainly African and European blood, and possibly something of the East.

the 15th century and for more than a century Portuguese survivors of shipwrecks added genes to the mix.

After the Dutch settled in the Cape in 1652 it became the major way station for trading ships sailing between Europe and India, with people of many nations pausing or staying there. Among their descendants are the many people in Cape Town today who have the unusual combination of blue eyes, blond hair and brown skin. Slaves and refugees from Indonesia and Malaya intermarried with other races, and their blood runs in the veins of Afrikaners.

French Huguenots came and settled, followed by immigrants from England and Germany. One Englishman, John Dunn, took a flock of Zulu wives in the 19th century and fathered an entire sub-tribe. Diamonds and gold lured Scots, Irish, Americans, Australians and many more. Lithuanians and Estonians fled from Hitler. Czechoslovakian settlers brought with them their beads, giving the Ndebele people new ideas for

LEFT The bonnet worn by this Northern Cape woman reflects her Dutch or Afrikaans ancestry. The language of the Coloureds, people of mixed blood, is Afrikaans.

ABOVE This general dealer's store in Pilgrim's Rest, Mpumalanga, is filled with memorabilia of the gold rush days in the late 19th century, next to modern products.

FACING A Shangaan woman in the Limpopo Province plucks emperor moth caterpillars from a mopane tree to be dried and then fried or powdered into stew.

RIGHT Anything goes on Johannesburg's sidewalks, including a lunchtime snack of dried mopane worms washed down with Coke.

FACING The blue and white cloak worn by this woman shows that she is a member of one of South Africa's numerous Christian sects. She is in a Johannesburg shop that sells "muti", traditional medicines.

ABOVE The people of the Richtersveld, largely of Khoi descent, eke out a living from their small herds of goats and by making handicrafts such as scarves.

decoration. Swedes came to fight alongside the Afrikaners and their missionaries taught the Zulus how to make tapestries and ceramics. French missionaries left French inflexions in the Basotho language.

Today mosques, churches, synagogues and Hindu temples within sight of each other testify to the mixture. In city streets people wear many styles of dress – saris, smart suits, the massive bead and brass anklets and neck rings of the Ndebele, the wide flat headdresses of the Zulu women, the colourful Basotho blankets. They talk in any one of a dozen languages, or a medley of languages, with many people able to switch easily from one language to another.

Although South Africans generally define themselves as white or black, English or Afrikaner, Zulu or Sotho or some other black group, Catholic or Protestant or Hindu or ancestor worshipper, and remain culturally distinct, the social divisions are becoming increasingly blurred. At work and play they are, in the end, all South Africans.

RIGHT The Western Cape's resorts and beaches are drawing more tourists every year. These visitors are at Keurbooms on the Garden Route.

LEFT Firewood is scarce in the dry Northern Cape. This Topnaar woman probably had to walk miles to collect her load.

BELOW The Xhosa people of the Eastern Cape inhabit some of South Africa's coolest countryside, hence the blanket and jerseys.

RIGHT Three generations of a Topnaar family — grandmother, daughter and granddaughter — sit on the doorstep of their Richtersveld home. Like other Khoi people, the Topnaar have adopted the Afrikaans language, dress and many customs.

BELOW South Africa's hope for the future is that children of all races will reject the prejudices of the past. Such sights are commonplace today.

RIGHT At a roadside in the middle of nowhere in KwaZulu/Natal an enterprising Zulu woman has built a stall offering a pot-pourri of wares.

ABOVE *With the dismantling of apartheid, people of all races started to enjoy each other's company as at this light-hearted evening barbecue.*

ABOVE *Education is the black population's biggest single need. These students are among the few lucky enough to have reached university level.*

RIGHT *A lunchtime chess game in Johannesburg's Joubert Park, like the new South Africa, has no race barriers.*

RIGHT *The pop group Amapondo perform at one of the venues along the Victoria and Albert Waterfront in Cape Town.*

BELOW Fishing brings many visitors to the Lake St Lucia complex of game reserves in northern KwaZulu/Natal, as do its warm climate and golden sunsets.

RIGHT A game ranger cools his feet in the river after taking a party of visitors on a long day's hiking in the Umfolozi reserve in KwaZulu/Natal.

LEFT The 1987–96 "Puppets Against Aids" project, here in action in the streets of Alexandra near Johannesburg, was part of a nationwide education programme to combat the disease.

ABOVE There is no better way to see the full spread and beauty of the early morning landscape than from the basket of a balloon, a fast-growing sport.

LEFT A popular pastime is to savour the country's riverine beauty from a canoe. The lily-covered water here is the Riviersonderend ("River Without End") in the Western Cape.

LEFT *For the more daring there are challenging rock climbs throughout the country. This cliff is at Waterval Boven ("Upper Waterfall") on the Escarpment in Mpumalanga.*

BELOW (LEFT) *South Africa has earned high ranking for its cricket prowess since it was re-admitted into international competition. This is a Castle Currie Cup match.*

BELOW *Trout fishing, mostly for rainbow trout and occasionally for brown trout, is one of the most popular ways for city dwellers to relax. Fishing rights are highly sought after and costly.*

LEFT A surfer skilfully "shoots a tube" off a beach in KwaZulu/Natal, which hosts the Gunston 500 and several other contests that draw international stars.

BELOW Rugby spectators erupt with joy as a touchdown is scored. Rugby is the most popular sport among the white community.

ABOVE South Africa and India compete at polo, a game which has been played for many years in South Africa but which was frustrated by the lack of competition during the time of its sporting isolation.

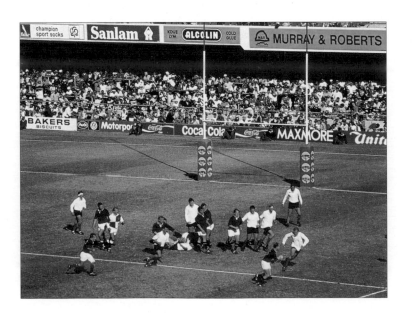

LEFT The Newlands rugby stadium in Cape Town is one of the top four in the country, and the one where the game is most likely to be played in wet, muddy conditions.

LEFT *Bloubergstrand ("Blue Mountain Beach") on the northern end of Table Bay is a favourite windsurfing venue, the wind sweeping off thousands of kilometres of open Atlantic.*

RIGHT *Catamaran teams prepare their craft for a competition at The Strand, False Bay.*

BELOW *South Africa's world class long-distance runner, Elana Meyer, leads a race in Durban wearing her trademark smile.*

9

ARCHITECTURE

IN ITS BROADEST SENSE, architecture in South Africa dates back to centuries before external influences arrived with the colonizers and settlers from Europe and the East. Simple mud, grass or reed homes have been the style among African peoples for thousands of years, but as recently as 1990 evidence was found of an early society with considerably more advanced building techniques.

At Thulamela in the far north of the Kruger National Park archaeologists have uncovered and painstakingly reconstructed the large, thick, well-built, dry-stone walls of a sizeable fortress settlement that flourished here between the 14th and 17th centuries. Smelting equipment and sophisticated gold, copper and iron artefacts indicate that it was an outpost of the large Monomotapa kingdom established by the Rozwi people, the builders of Great Zimbabwe.

When the Dutch occupied the Cape in 1652 they built a wood and earthen fort but later replaced it with the Cape Town Castle, the country's oldest building, completed in 1679. It is in the style typical of the times, a five-pointed star with bastions at the corners. Thereafter the first truly local architecture evolved – the Cape Dutch

FACING A Zulu hut made of tightly woven grass, with a low doorway and a hard-beaten earthen floor, is surprisingly cosy but these traditional homes are giving way to square or round mud-walled thatched houses and brick buildings.

RIGHT *This is a typical stone-built Karoo farmhouse, with its windpump, water reservoir and screened stoep. The stoep's curved corrugated-iron roof indicates that the house is over a century old.*

ABOVE *Log cabins, like this one at Cape Vidal in KwaZulu/Natal, are fairly new to South Africa but, with the expansion of the timber industry and effective treatment against termites, more are now being built.*

LEFT *Built in the Cape Peninsula's Constantia Valley, Klein Constantia is the homestead of a well-known vineyard and one of the oldest and most beautiful Cape Dutch houses.*

ABOVE This mill, with its loft, is at Elim mission in the Western Cape. The old flatbed wagon in the foreground is now a rarity, but such wagons were used on farms as recently as the 1950s.

RIGHT The traditional round thatched huts of the Xhosa people in the Eastern Cape are slowly giving way to modern characterless square homes with corrugated-iron roofs.

ABOVE Mostert's Mill in Cape Town's Mowbray suburb, a well-known landmark to thousands of people driving to and from work along Rhodes Drive, was built in 1795 and restored in 1936.

LEFT Laundry makes a splash of colour against the clean whitewashed homes in Arniston, a fishing village near Cape Agulhas.

RIGHT The old print house and neighbouring buildings in Pilgrim's Rest date from the late 19th century gold rush. On the inside, in a style borrowed from British India, the walls and corrugated-iron roofs are lined with wood.

BELOW Behind the expensive brick homes in Soweto's "Beverly Hills" lies the soulless monotony of mass housing and, in the background, hostel blocks built for single men – a legacy of apartheid.

LEFT Cities are fast being ringed by "informal settlements", a euphemism for vast slums of shacks with few services and crowded with rural migrants.

ABOVE The polyglot mass of apartment blocks in Hillbrow, on the left, overlooks Johannesburg's high-rise central business district.

ABOVE This mass building project, one of many in South Africa's urban areas, is designed to provide jobs as well as housing.

RIGHT Some building developments, though monotonous, provide homes of a fairly good standard, such as this one on Mitchell's Plain in the Western Cape.

ABOVE Decent housing and services will greatly enhance this little girl's prospects in life. With high unemployment levels, the challenge is to provide homes of reasonable quality at a cost people can afford.

ABOVE *Gold Reef City, near Johannesburg, recaptures the British colonial building styles common in mining towns at the turn of the century.*

ABOVE (RIGHT) *San Lameer near Durban provides luxurious water-side homes for the wealthy to enjoy their boating and other pleasures.*

ABOVE *The intricate "brookie lace" trellis work and down-curved roof over the stoep of a house in Somerset East, Eastern Cape, were popular architectural features in the 19th century.*

LEFT *The controversial Ponte apartment block, in the middle, dominates Johannesburg's crowded skyline. On the far left is the huge Carlton Centre.*

RIGHT This Cape Dutch house is one of 32 historic buildings in the 200-year-old town of Tulbagh, Western Cape, which were fully restored after being destroyed in an earthquake in 1969.

BELOW The glass walls of the Forest Lodge in the Phinda resource centre, KwaZulu/Natal, give visitors an extraordinary sense of being among the fauna and flora of the game reserve.

LEFT In a classic old Victorian home in Prince Albert Hamlet, meticulously pointed brick offsets the intricate trelliswork.

LEFT Along Cape Town's Victoria and Albert Waterfront, in the lap of Table Mountain, are some fine old buildings, all recently refurbished.

RIGHT Bright colours redeem the otherwise plain wooden changing rooms at St James beach on False Bay, Cape Town.

ABOVE *A major challenge in the new South Africa is to provide all homes with adequate electricity, water and sewage services.*

LEFT *The Dutch Reformed Church in George, Western Cape, was built in the 1830s in the classic cross shape, with thick earthen walls. The rococo gable and round tower are unusual features.*

RIGHT *Most modern architecture in Johannesburg emulates foreign trends and uses high-tech materials, as in this "windowless" office block in the city centre.*

RIGHT *The centrepiece of Pietermaritzburg's many Victorian buildings is its city hall, burned down in 1898 and rebuilt three years later. It is said to be the biggest all-brick building in the Southern Hemisphere.*

ABOVE *The Anglo American Corporation's high-rise glass structure, in Diagonal Street, Johannesburg, is suggestive of a cut diamond.*

BELOW *An eclectic mishmash of buildings crowds the Durban beachfront, most of them designed for the tourist trade which, after the harbour, is the city's major source of revenue.*

RIGHT *The Palace of the Lost City hotel and casino in the Northwest province is a fantasy conceived by American and South African architects which incorporates aspects of several cultures.*

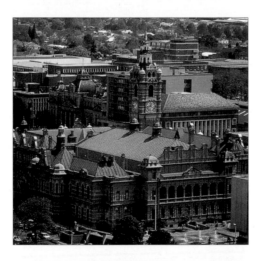

ABOVE The smooth, glassy lines of one of the country's largest hotels soar from the sidewalks of downtown Johannesburg. The city now abounds with buildings of this type.

LEFT In Polokwane, capital of the Limpopo Province and service centre for 6 million people, the new library building was designed to include an art gallery exhibiting South African works.

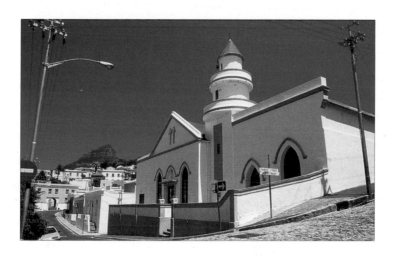

LEFT This small mosque, with its two-tiered muezzin tower, and a plain gable reminiscent of the Cape Dutch style, is in the delightful Bo-Kaap ("Above Cape") Malay quarter of Cape Town, an area now conserved as a national monument.

 # INDEX